Origins

Animal Conflicts

Steve Parker

Contents

OXFORD
UNIVERSITY PRESS

Struggle for survival

It's tough in the wild. Animals face many different dangers. **Predators** want to eat them. **Invaders** try to take over their homes. **Rivals** aim to be boss of the group or to take their mates at **breeding** time. Their babies need protection from predators and accidents. Sometimes they have to fight to survive.

A praying mantis jabs a victim with its spiky front legs.

Buffaloes push and shove each other.

Avoiding conflict

Animals do not look for danger on purpose. They only get into **conflicts** when they really have to. That's because if a wild animal suffers even a small injury, it could mean big trouble. The injury might get worse and threaten the animal's life. So wild creatures try to avoid fights whenever they can.

Male peacocks try to outdo each other by showing their colourful feathers.

A rhino will lower its head before a charge to make its nose horn look big.

Attack and defence

Animals have different ways of defending themselves. Before they get into a fight they often give warnings. Each animal tries to make itself look as big, strong and dangerous as possible. It might rear up, puff out its fur or feathers, jump about or make sounds like roars, hisses or growls. All this makes the animal seem fierce and scary.

Teeth

Teeth are mainly used for eating but, in a conflict, animals such as dogs open their mouths to show their teeth. They also growl, put their ears back and make the hair on their neck stand up. This scares away other animals.

Claws

Some animals use their claws to scratch or slash rivals or predators and to defend themselves against danger.

An African wild dog bares its teeth.

Hooves

Animals like zebras, giraffes and deer can kick out strongly against predators with their hard hooves.

Horns

Many animals have horns. Antelopes and gazelles have sharp horns that grow longer each year. By moving their heads up and down, they make the horns look dangerous.

Tails

Animals also use their tails for defence. A rattlesnake shakes its tail to make a buzzing sound. This warns other animals: 'Stay away, I have a **poisonous** bite!'

I'm poisonous!

Some animals have weapons that are chemical substances – poisons or **venoms**. These are for catching prey, for self-defence and for threatening rivals. Often the animal does not have to use them in a conflict. Just showing its poisonous fangs or venomous sting is enough to make an opponent turn away.

Warning colours

Some poisonous animals are brightly coloured. These warning colours tell other creatures to stay away because of the poison.

Poison dart frog

Tail stings

Wasps, bees, scorpions and other creatures have a dangerous sting in the tail. For more on bee stings see page 26.

African yellow-leg scorpion

Venomous darts

Some kinds of sea-snails have a small hard dart, like a tiny spear, to stab powerful poison into a victim.

Coneshell sea-snail

Poisonous fangs

Several kinds of snakes have a poisonous bite, with long thin stabbing teeth called fangs.

Rattlesnake

Horrible spits and sprays

Some animals spit or spray their poison. This can cause the other creature great pain, skin damage and can even make them blind.

A skunk defends itself by spraying a horrible scent.

King cobra vs mongoose

The king cobra preys on the mongoose. The mongoose would also like to make a meal of the snake. But how do they match up?

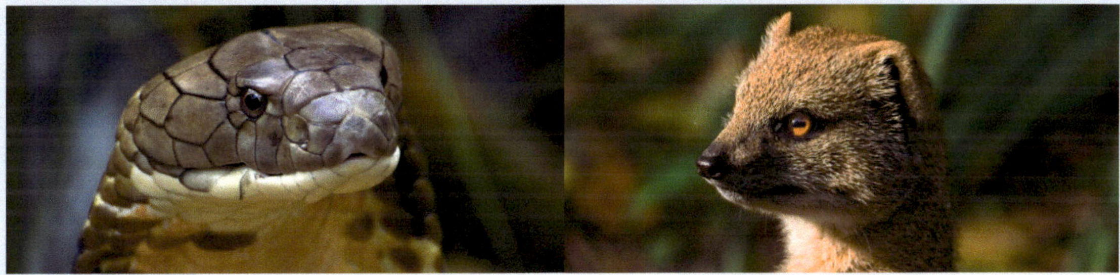

	King cobra	**Mongoose**
Size	4 m long, weighs 6 kg	70 cm long, weighs 2 kg
Strengths	Very fast. Long fangs. Deadly bite. Excellent eyesight. Body protected by hard scales.	Very fast. Leaps quickly. Thick fur protects skin. High tolerance to cobra venom.
Weaknesses	Long body and tail to attack. Cannot jump.	No poison. Teeth are not very long.
Main tactics	Watches and waits. Strikes (bites) at speed to jab in poison.	Moves and 'dances' around cobra. Tries to leap on to the back of its neck, biting hard.

Show fights

Many animal conflicts are pretend fights. The animals show off but never touch each other. This way they are less likely to be injured, which is very important for a wild creature. A broken bone, a **sprain** or even a small cut might prevent the animal moving around or feeding. If an injury gets infected with germs, it can cause serious illness, even death. There are no animal hospitals in the wild!

Rituals

Some animals engage in **ritual** behaviour when they are in a conflict. Their actions are similar to what they normally do, but other animals know they mean trouble.

Angry gorilla

Normal action:

Gorillas often bend or shake branches to feed on fruits and leaves.

Ritual behaviour:

When a gorilla is under threat, it shakes branches much harder. It also opens its mouth to show its big teeth, roars, slaps its chest and stamps its heels.

Frilly jumper

Normal action:

The frilled lizard often jumps into tree branches to feed.

Ritual behaviour:

A frilled lizard in danger jumps about even more than normal. It spreads out the wide frill of skin around its neck, opens its mouth and hisses to scare away enemies.

Scared-ee cat

Normal action:

Cats fluff up their fur when they are cold, to keep warm.

Ritual behaviour:

A scared cat fluffs out its fur to look bigger and fiercer. It folds its ears back, waves its tail, hisses and extends its claws.

QUIZ

Answers on page 32!

Which of these animals hisses if it gets into a conflict?

Cat

Snake

Madagascar cockroach

Toad

Crocodile

Get off my patch!

Many animals stay in one area known as their **territory**. They live in the territory and feed and raise their young there. Territories can range in size from a small garden for a robin, to many hills and valleys for an eagle or a tiger.

The best territories have plenty of food and safe places to rest, hide and raise young. Sometimes an animal will have to defend its territory against an invader who wants the area for itself. Many animal conflicts are over territories.

Robins are very territorial. They will squawk, peck and flap at each other to defend their territory.

The same kind

Usually, only animals of the same species have territorial disputes. For example, a robin might fight another robin over a territory, but it wouldn't fight a blackbird, a mouse or a bat. These other creatures live in different ways and eat different foods, so they are not a threat to the robin.

Male hippos roar and bite each other to take control of a length of river.

A dragonfly's territory is around a pond or stream. It flaps its wings at other dragonflies to chase them away.

Male lions make loud, frightening roars. They are telling lions in nearby prides to stay out of their territory.

I'm the boss!

Some creatures are social. This means they live together in groups. For example, ants live in big nests, elephants live in herds, and there are flocks of birds and swarms of insects.

Animal groups often have a leader – the **dominant** member of the group. This can cause conflict because sometimes others in the group want to be the leader instead. If they cannot beat the leader, they might fight others to be second or third in charge.

These two male elephant seals are fighting to see who will be in charge.

Pecking order

Having a leader, a second in charge and so on, is known as a 'pecking order' because it was first studied in farmyard hens. The boss, or dominant hen, pecks all the others to keep them in their place. The second in charge pecks all the other hens but not the leader. Bottom of the list is the hen that is pecked by all the others but does not peck back.

Two leaders

A wolf pack has two leaders – the alpha male and alpha female. They are the only ones that have babies, called cubs. The other pack members help to raise the cubs.

Only the alpha wolves can mate in a wolf pack.

First choice

Why do animals fight for control of their group? One reason is that the leader has the first choice of food. When a troop (a group) of monkeys goes to a new tree, the leader pushes the others out of the way and eats the biggest, tastiest fruits.

Another reason is that the leader can select the best resting place. A group of lobsters will fight for the best caves, cracks and **crevices**, where they can hide and wait for prey. These battles get so fierce that legs and claws can be nipped off!

A monkey enjoying a banana.

A lobster ready to defend its chosen spot on a rock.

The group leader also has the first pick of a mate at breeding time. Naked mole-rats live underground. Only the female queen and up to three males breed. The other males help to dig tunnels and collect food. But they do not mate with females or have **offspring**.

Naked mole-rats use their long front teeth to dig underground tunnels.

In most animal groups, the males are the leaders. But bonobo chimpanzees live in female-led groups. The females decide where to go, what to eat, when to rest and where to sleep.

A female bonobo is the boss of her group.

Food fight!

All creatures need to eat, so sometimes they fight over food. Before starting a food fight each animal must decide if it can get another meal more easily. Is the food worth fighting for? Can it scare the other animal away or will it have to overpower the rival?

Hungry vultures jostle for position around a carcass.

Lion vs hyena

A big animal like a zebra or wildebeest is a huge feast for a group of lions. But hungry hyenas are fierce rivals for the meat.

	Lion	**Hyena**
Size	2 m long, weighs 200 kg	1.5 m long, weighs 50 kg
Strengths	Big and powerful. Huge teeth and claws.	Works well in a group. Does not tire easily.
Weaknesses	Tires easily.	Teeth, jaws and claws are smaller than lion's.
Main tactics	Growls, roars and tries to bite.	Keeps pestering the lion until it leaves.

Hyenas chase off a lion that is competing for a share of a kill.

Rivals at breeding time

Breeding time is very important for all animals. Males will often show off to females in order to get a mate. Each male tries to do better than the other males. This is when conflicts can happen.

Every autumn, deer gather to breed. The males, called stags, snort and toss their heads to show off their big antlers. They clash antlers, push and twist. It's a test of power and strength. Eventually the strongest stag wins and gets to mate with the females. The clash of antlers is known as rutting.

Male birds of paradise try to outdo one another by putting on the best display. Each one shows off its colourful feathers, makes loud squawks and does a dance.

Narwhals are a type of whale. The male narwhal has a long, pointed tooth called a tusk. In the mating season, males clash their tusks, like they are having a sword fight.

Leks

Sometimes male animals go to one place to show off to females. The place is called a 'lek'. Male black grouse collect at their lek, strut around, fan their tails, jump up and down and make loud calls.

QUIZ

Answers on page 32!

Match the names of the animals to the names of the male and female.

1) Fox
2) Deer
3) Whale
4) Bird of paradise

a) Stag and hind or doe
b) Bull and cow
c) Cock and hen
d) Dog and vixen

It's only courtship

Before animals mate they need to check to see if their partner is strong and healthy, so that their offspring will also be fit and strong. This process of getting to know their partner is called courtship.

Sometimes courtship can look like a conflict as many animals test each other by pushing, scratching and biting. But no harm is done.

A female jaguar bites a male jaguar.

The male rainbow fish darts around the female when courting. He flaps his fins and flicks her with his tail.

Courting dolphins slap each other with their tails, prod with their noses and bump their sides together.

A male spider has to be careful during courtship as the female is larger and may decide to eat him!

Beetle vs beetle

	Male stag beetle	**Female stag beetle**
Size	7 cm long, weighs 3 g	4 cm long, weighs 2 g
Strengths	Bigger than female. Huge antler-like jaws.	Faster than male. Powerful legs. Strong jaw muscles.
Weaknesses	Jaw muscles are very weak.	Smaller-sized body.
Main tactics	Jumps on to female to weigh her down.	Females are strong and quick and may push the male away.

Protective parents

Baby animals are usually small, weak and unable to move fast or defend themselves. All kinds of hungry predators are ready to make meals of them. So being a parent and protecting the young is very important.

Animals are always ready to defend their babies and will even give up their own lives to save their offspring. Predators know this so they don't always take the risk against a protective parent.

A killdeer bird protects her eggs by taking a defensive pose. She puffs up her body to make herself look as strong as possible.

Parent power

- When killer whales attack a baby grey whale, the mother grey whale tries to keep her enormous body between her baby and the killers.

- If a cougar (mountain lion) tries to eat a baby bear, the mother bear will roar and swipe with her huge paws and claws.

- If a leopard gets too near a baby elephant, the other elephants in the herd will charge with loud trumpeting sounds.

- When a hawk attempts to take an owl chick from its nest, the mother owl spreads her wings, pecks with her sharp beak and scratches with her long talons (claws).

- Few animals would try to steal a baby alligator from its mother. She protects it in her open mouth!

QUIZ

Answers on page 32!

Match the names of the animals with the names of their young.

1) Alligator	a) Hatchling
2) Owl	b) Cub
3) Whale	c) Chick
4) Bear	d) Calf

Helping others

To avoid a serious conflict, some animals live in groups so they can protect each other. Together they can watch out for predators and invaders. If one animal spots danger, it can warn the others. A predator is also less likely to risk attacking a whole group of animals.

Baboons are big, strong monkeys. They watch, sniff and listen for trouble such as a leopard or eagle. At the first sign of a threat, they open their mouths to show their long teeth and scream. They come together in a line, ready to attack the attacker.

Helping mum and dad

When birds called white-fronted bee-eaters are partly grown, they become 'helpers' for their parents. They gather food for the parents' new chicks and even fight off hawks and snakes who try to eat the chicks.

White-fronted bee-eaters look after each other in family groups.

Too many to attack

Zebras always watch for enemies such as lions, leopards and hyenas. If one zebra detects danger, it brays and alerts all the others. The whole herd races towards the enemy, who is then in great danger of being knocked over and trampled.

When zebras run as a herd, their stripes can confuse their enemies, making it difficult for their enemies to see an individual zebra to attack.

Losing life for others

In some animal conflicts, members of a group may attack a predator – even though they will almost certainly die. Why do they risk their lives? Usually it is because all of the group members are related. So even if they die, they are helping their family to live.

If a bear tries to steal honey from a bees' nest, the bees sting it. But as each bee's sting jabs the bear's skin, the sting tears off the rear of the bee's body. The bee soon dies.

A close-up of a bee's sting.

Soldiers on guard

In a termite nest, the soldier termites have much bigger jaws than the worker termites. These soldiers bite any animal disturbing the nest, even a giant anteater trying to eat them!

Giant anteater vs termite

The giant anteater is thousands of times bigger than the ants and termites it eats. But it suffers so many tiny termite bites that it does not stay for long.

	Giant anteater	**Soldier termite**
Size	2.5 m long, weighs 50 kg	5 mm long, weighs 100th of a gram
Strengths	Huge and powerful. Massive claws. Long, sticky tongue.	Many thousands in number. Sharp jaws.
Weaknesses	Only one in number.	Very small.
Main tactics	Licks up lots of ants as fast as possible, then escapes.	Bites many times, as hard as possible, until it is eaten.

Animals at war

Most animal conflicts are between just two creatures or just a few. Really big battles with many animals are rare but they do happen. The reasons include fighting for more food, a better nest site, a safer place to live or a bigger territory.

Chimpanzee groups have fierce battles. If the chief males in one troop think that they are bigger and stronger than their neighbours, then they 'go to war'. If their neighbours resist, they may be killed and even eaten.

An angry chimpanzee.

Siamangs are a kind of ape. They live in families. If one family strays into the territory of another family, there may be a conflict. All of the members, even the youngsters, get involved. They call loudly and shake the branches. They even bite and scratch, until one family backs off.

Siamang

MILLIONS DEAD

Army ants or driver ants have no nests. They march through the forest and stop each night in a different place. If two armies meet, they bite, sting and fight each other. Thousands or even millions might die.

JUNGL

At this ti
mar

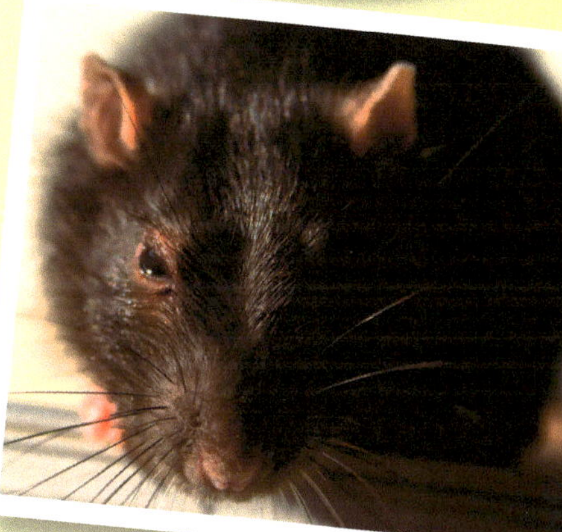

Rats usually form fighting packs due to lack of food or being too crowded together.

QUIZ

Match the names of these animals to the groups they form.

Answers on page 32!

1) Rats	a) Family
2) Chimpanzees	b) Pack
3) Driver ants	c) Troop
4) Siamangs	d) Army

Fight to the death

A predator's aim is to catch, kill and eat its prey. It does not manage this every time it hunts, however. A tiger catches its prey only about one hunt in ten, so prey have a good chance of escape.

Sperm whale vs giant squid

The world's biggest fight happens in the deep ocean between the world's largest predator, the sperm whale, and the giant squid.

	Sperm whale	**Giant squid**
Size	20 m long, weighs 50 000 kg	13 m long, weighs 3 000 kg
Strengths	Massive size. Powerful jaws. Lots of teeth. Strong swimmer.	Tentacles with strong suckers and sharp hooks. Sharp-beaked mouth. Moves fast.
Weaknesses	Cannot twist or turn fast. Must surface to breathe air.	No shell or other protection.
Main tactics	Uses its large mouth to bite then swallow the squid.	Scrapes, scratches and bites.

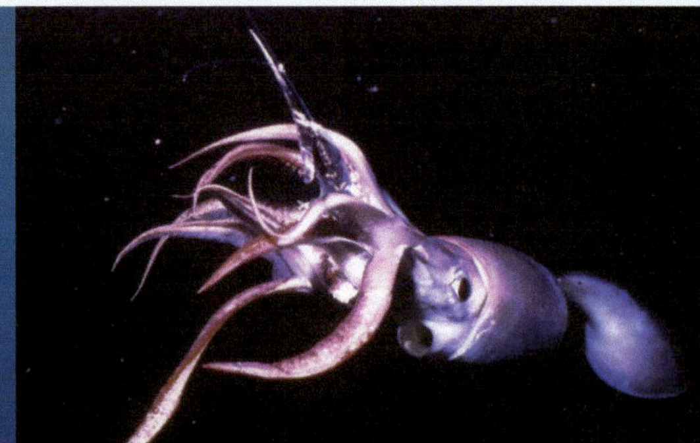

Glossary

breeding	when two parent animals mate to make babies
conflict	a fight, struggle or disagreement
crevice	a narrow gap in a rock or building
dominant	the strongest member of a group
invader	someone who comes into where you live and tries to take it over
offspring	an animal's (or person's) children
poisonous	a substance that can cause harm or even death
predator	an animal that kills other animals (its prey) for food
ritual	a series of actions, often repeated, that is used in a ceremony
rival	someone that you compete against
sprain	to injure part of the body by twisting it
territory	an area of land that an animal or group of animals lives in
venom	a poisonous fluid produced by an animal

Index

QUIZ ANSWERS

Page 9:
All of them!

Page 13:
1b) A pride of lions
2d) A flock of sheep
3a) A herd of horses
4c) A swarm of eels

Page 19:
1d) Fox: dog and vixen
2a) Deer: stag and hind or doe
3b) Whale: bull and cow
4c) Bird of paradise: cock and hen

Page 23:
1a) Alligator hatchling
2c) Owl chick
3d) Whale calf
4b) Bear cub

Page 29:
1b) A pack of rats
2c) A troop of chimpanzees
3d) An army of driver ants
4a) A family of siamangs